AGE UNLIMITED

Exploring Employment Barriers for Older Workers

Catherine S. Shrubsole

PROHASKA HAMPTON
PUBLISHING

Prohaska Hampton Publishing
Brisbane, Australia

Published in Australia in 2018 by Catherine S. Shrubsole,
Prohaska Hampton Publishing

Email: prohaskahampton@gmail.com

© Catherine S. Shrubsole 2018

ISBN 9780648142706 (paperback)

A catalogue record for this
book is available from the
National Library of Australia

NATIONAL
LIBRARY
OF AUSTRALIA

Disclaimer

This book is distributed as an information source only to sup-
plement the reader's own knowledge and judgment and is not
intended to replace professional legal advice. The materials and
information in this book are based on published information
sources and may be subject to change. While all reasonable efforts
have been made to publish correct data and information, readers
should make their own assessment and verification of the materials and information in this book. The author cannot be held
responsible for any claims arising from the use of this book or any
accidental errors or omissions. All reasonable efforts have been
made to acknowledge and correctly attribute information sources.
Contact the author to report errors or updates so that they can be
corrected in subsequent editions of this publication.

To lifelong learners

What a piece of work is a man!
How noble in reason! How infinite in faculty!
In form and moving how express and admirable!
In action how like an angel! In apprehension how like a god!

William Shakespeare
Hamlet, Act II, Scene 2, 303–312

CONTENTS

Preface

I have participated in countless job interviews and performance reviews, from both sides of the table.

As an HR practitioner, people leader and recruitment consultant, I have joined decision-making processes to find good and talented employees and design ways to retain their valuable, and often scarce, knowledge, skills and experience. Questions abound about how to align diversity and fairness with organisational effectiveness. Having been a contractor and a job seeker on more than one occasion – in addition to being an 'officially' older worker – I am also interested in the steps older workers can take to overcome employment barriers when looking for a job, accessing training, remaining in the workforce, or seeking a new challenge.

With all of this in mind, I wanted to investigate the research on the perceptions of, and reality about, older workers. Are older workers a good bet or bad news? What are the myths and stereotypes, and what is the factual basis for these perceptions? If employers' issues and concerns about older workers are genuine and factually based, then can older workers take their own actions to sustain their employment?

It is no surprise that older workers believe they have been unfairly treated in their employment because of their age. The concept of 'older' itself depends very much on who is doing the conceptualising. Ages of forty-five years, fifty-five years, and sixty-five years are all used to define an older worker across Australian legislation, and such varying perceptions of 'older' are found in many similarly developed economies.

Thirty year-olds think that the age of fifty-five years is 'older', while fifty-five year-olds tend to think that 'older' is a descriptive word not related to a number such as chronological age. With longer life expectancy in Australia and rising community expectations that we will work for longer, age-related employment barriers are likely to affect all of us eventually.

I have a deep wish to learn from the best, make sense of the world and find innovative solutions to real problems. In realising this I have been fortunate to build on my university studies, with a Bachelor of Commerce and a Bachelor of Arts (Honours) in Psychology from the University of Queensland, and a Master of Employment Relations, and over twenty years' experience in human resources in both the private and public sectors.

My goal is to make the relevant research about age-related barriers to employment more accessible to decision-makers and workers. In this way, we can all learn and create more effective organisations and more meaningful work for everyone.

Whether you are a people leader, an older worker or a practitioner, I look forward to sharing this journey with you.

Catherine S. Shrubsole
December 2017

Ageing creates as much
as it casts away.

Introduction

Sharing the Journey

We are all ageing all the time.

Expectant parents delightfully count the days and weeks of growth and development in utero. Families gather for a child's first birthday. We stake social, cultural, and ritual milestones on age: school age, teenage, driving age, voting age, drinking age.

Eighteenth and twenty-first birthdays are typical gateways to adulthood. From then onwards, however, we observe fewer age markers. The random exceptions are reports of common activities made remarkable by the age of the participant. Think about the number of times that driving, diving, parachuting, winning a prize, and sometimes even taking a long walk are of public interest only because participants are of a 'certain age'. Beyond that, we seem to have ceased celebrating ageing.

As people mature, perhaps we are too involved in living to peg milestones to something as commonplace as age. We are immersed in working, rearing, creating, building, thinking, writing, solving, innovating, philosophising, loving, planning, exercising, caring, teaching, mourning... Perhaps the number of years on the planet is meaningless in marking or measuring achievements or disappointments.

While we advertise an eighteenth birthday, the forty-eighth birthday is usually a private affair. We post twenty-first birthday banners but, thirty years later, a fifty-first birthday is almost a secret. Is it that we revere and celebrate other aspects of a mature life, or is less said about age the better for an older person and, in particular, an older worker? Such workers may be older and wiser, but are they limited by their age?

An overwhelming volume of research and data about older workers and employment stretches back for decades, both in Australia and across the globe. The research examines negative stereotypes, age discrimination, legal processes for redress, self-help advice, the business case for age diversity, the social-moral argument for employment equity, and so on. Researchers, governments, and analysts are engaged worldwide in identifying issues, validating data, and proposing and testing recommendations. The problem for employers, people leaders, HR practitioners and older workers themselves is accessing and synthesising this mass of information in ways that can be profitably applied in commercial and working life.

The objective of this book is to make research and data more accessible to decision-makers and to add to robust conversations about effectively managing the range of talent in the organisation's workforce. The goal is to inform the employment relations debate by reviewing, interpreting and, especially, bringing together the relevant research on employment barriers for older workers. Much of the analysis relies on the published research and data from the ten years between 2006 and 2016. While the numbers will change over time – as we all do – this book draws out general trends and lays the foundation for action-planning for employers and older workers.

The age-related barriers to employment and the recommendations for employers outlined in this book refer specifically to Australian demographics and employment relations, but many of the takeaways can be usefully applied in other labour markets with a similar socio-economic structure, where the challenges facing older workers will be comparable[1,2]. For example, the model for a worker as an able-bodied male was enshrined early in Australia's national history and became the norm. This model marginalises women working outside the home, older and disabled workers, sole-parent workers and multi-generational family work groups. The model is still operating – often implicitly – today, as is the case in many places around the world.

To place the data in a context, this book explores definitions of 'older worker' and describes the demographics of the Australian workforce. In 2014, in Australia life expectancy at birth was over eighty years[3]. With longer life expectancy, people's working life is predicted to extend into their seventies and even into their eighties. Therefore, most workers will be at risk of age discrimination and face barriers to sustaining their employment at some point in their working life.

These changing and ageing demographics give rise to exploring the basis for age-related barriers to employment and dismantling them wherever it is appropriate. This book presents relevant negative and positive stereotypes and seeks to explore the reality of these views. From an equity approach to disadvantage, all workers are entitled to a fair share of the benefits of employment. Looking at the business case for workforce diversity, employing a wide range of workers aids competitive advantage and contributes to organisational effectiveness. Supporting both equity and diversity approaches many economic advantages stem from broader workforce participation, including a deeper taxation base and reduced public funding for aged income assistance.

Research indicates that employers perceive older workers to be costly, with reduced performance due to out-of-date skills, poor health and declining physical and mental abilities, and provide a low return on investment in training and development. While these negative perceptions of older workers are not always true nor can they be automatically applied to all older workers, the negative take on older workers persists in society and in many organisations. Even the positive views that employers hold of older workers are based on older workers' compliant work behaviours rather than their performance at work. Negative stereotypes of older workers and an organisational context that assumes (and may create) performance deficits in older workers both impact employment-related age discrimination.

Research makes clear that negative perceptions of older workers are widely-held in society and among employers. However, the research does not support that negative stereotypes of older workers represent the reality for all older workers, all the time.

In some cases, threats of negative stereotypes and discrimination in the workplace are self-fulfilling – these negative opinions can produce work environments that lead to reduced performance by older workers. In other cases, non-productive behaviours of an older worker are limited to the special circumstances of that individual worker and it is not reasonable to generalise to all older workers. Just because some older workers, for example, have health conditions that at times prevent a commitment to full-time work, this is not an indicator of the attitudes and abilities, needs and wishes of all older workers.

Within the pages of this book, we will explore and identify the factual basis (if any) for negative perceptions and stereotypes in relation to older workers. The idea behind this approach is to help employers, people leaders and practitioners to develop more inclusive policies and work practices to contribute to organisational effectiveness.

Determining any factual basis for negative perceptions will also help older workers with their argument. So armed with the facts, older workers may either implement their own development plans to lift their performance shortfalls, or make their own informed business case that addresses the flawed perceptions.

This book presents five takeaways from the published research and data:

1. Employers hold negative stereotypes that older workers are more costly than younger workers, have poorer health and declining physical and mental abilities, are poorly skilled, and resist learning.

2. Negative stereotypes do not always reflect reality, especially in considering any particular older worker, and a non-inclusive organisational context can adversely impact the performance of older workers.

3. Older workers have valuable organisation and job-related knowledge, life experience, work ethic, commitment, and learning ability.

4. Inclusive and flexible working practices, and targeted manager training can retain productive older workers in the workforce.

5. Older workers can sustain their employment through education, up-skilling, effective interpersonal skills, and being adaptable to change.

This book puts forward action points to overcome age-related barriers to the employment and retention of older workers. Employers can increase their talent resources by creating an organisation with more flexible practices. Employers can develop strategies to avoid placing older workers in work situations that diminish their performance, and train managers to recognise and optimise the contributions of older workers. Employers will then be well-placed to capitalise on the knowledge and experience of older workers.

There are hints for older workers – some active measures to sustain their own employment. Taking direct and personal action, older workers can implement a few strategies aimed to optimise their performance at work. Older workers can also take the initiative in their career development and in articulating the 'business case' for the contribution of older workers, to help sustain employment over their life cycle.

Ageing impacts all workers. The novice learns, and an expert may emerge. An apprentice is engaged and, with instruction, mentoring, practice and experience, a master craftswoman or craftsman may be made. An actor plays Romeo, but maybe not Lear … not yet. The memoir is more persuasively penned by the sage, and not the student. Over decades of experience, the developing professional can become the seasoned practitioner. When we are open and engaged, ageing creates as much as it casts away. Older workers can indeed be wiser, and age unlimited.

Perceptions of age change
with the age of the perceiver.

ONE

Setting the Scene

Examining Shifting Age Demographics

How we define 'older worker'

There are many mays to define what we mean by 'older worker' and those definitions can vary widely with the context and purpose, along with the perceptions of who, exactly, is seeking to define the term[1,2]. In reports released by the Australian Bureau of Statistics (ABS), an older worker is defined as being someone over fifty-five years of age[3]. The ABS defines prime age as between twenty-five and fifty-four years[4]. The prime age definition somewhat overlaps the softer 'prime working age' defined as between fifteen years and sixty-four years[5].

Legislative definitions are also context specific and policy dependent. Under the *Fair Work Act 2009* (Cwlth)[6], Australians are considered to be 'older' at forty-five years, and receive slightly more favourable notice on termination (s 117), but they must turn fifty-five years before they're eligible to statutorily request a flexible working arrangement (s 65). In 2016, sixty-five year-old Australians were old enough to be eligible for the age pension. On 1 July 2023, workers will need to be two years older (i.e. sixty-seven years) to qualify, and by 2035 may need to be three years older again to be old enough to be eligible for the age pension[7,8].

Perceptions of age change with the age of the perceiver, too. Thirty year-olds consider fifty year-olds to be 'older' while those who are fifty-five years and older think of the word 'older' as a description that does not necessarily relate to a specific number[9]. Older workers indicate that fifty years of age is the critical point where they tend to experience age discrimination[10]. Who is considered an older worker changes with the context, and when someone suddenly becomes an older worker does not occur at a fixed point in time.

Older workers in the Australian population

In December 2015, the Australian population was estimated at 24 million[11]. The median age of the population was a little over thirty-seven years[12]. In 2014, life expectancy for females at birth was eighty-four years and for males at birth was eighty years[13]. Females aged forty-five years in 2011 to 2013 could expect to live to eighty-five years, and males aged forty-five could expect to live to almost eighty-two years. In 2011 to 2013, this increased to eighty-seven years and eighty four years respectively for females and males aged sixty-five[14]. The Australian Treasury's Intergenerational Report (2015) forecast life expectancy at over ninety-five years by the year 2055[15]. With recorded and forecast increases in life expectancy, the need for governments, organisations and workers to sustain employment over the extended lifecycle is apparent from the perspective of: economic growth, commercial viability, and for older workers' independence and psychological well-being.

In order to realise the individual and social benefits of employment, older workers need to be able to participate in the workforce. In 2016, the workforce participation rate for the Australian population remained steady around 65 per cent[16].

Workforce participation for older workers has been increasing. From 1978–1979 to 2013–2014, participation in the workforce for older workers aged fifty-five to sixty-four years moved from 45.6 per cent to 63.8 per cent[15]. Increased participation of older workers is attributed to higher levels of education, delayed retirement, longer life expectancy, decreases in physically demanding work and new technologies[15,17]. The Productivity Commission's (2013) forecast to the year 2060 anticipated growth in the participation rate of older Australian workers[17]. However, this forecast growth was mostly in part-time and flexible work in the service sector, which may not align with older workers' preferred forms of work.

The Australian workforce demographic is also changing with respect to an increasing dependency rate. The dependency rate is the ratio of working-age people to every person sixty-five years or older. The Australian dependency rate in 2015 was 4.5 working-age people for every older Australian[17]. By the year 2055, the forecast dependency rate is 2.7 working-age people for every older Australian[15]. Unless participation rates are addressed, the Australian economy will be affected by decreased contribution to gross domestic product (GDP) and lower taxation revenues, and increased reliance on funding for income support[18,19,20,21,22]. Increasing the participation of older workers will help maintain the revenue base and moderate the need for public income support for the ageing, non-working population.

Older workers at work

There are multiple reasons to address age-related employment barriers. We may take the perspective of demographic impacts or equity in employment, look at the diversity business case for maximising the workforce contribution to organisations' effectiveness, or consider the work preferences of older workers themselves.

Australia has a history of considering fairness in employment and a more recent cultivated interest in managing diversity. Federal and state legislation provide protections for those who historically have been disadvantaged in employment. Such groups include women, older and disabled workers, and workers from a non-English-speaking background[23,24,25,26]. The *Age Discrimination Act 2004* (Cwlth)[24] makes it unlawful to discriminate in employment on the basis of age or the characteristics usually associated with that age (s 14). Legislation aligns with the equity view of a right to a fair share of society's benefits. People are protected and supported in seeking to earn a living and sustain their employment, regardless of their age.

From another perspective, maintaining a diverse workforce shifts the emphasis from redressing historical disadvantage. The managing diversity approach focuses instead on the benefits for organisational effectiveness from the full workforce contributions of a range of workers. The business case for managing diversity posits improved organisational effectiveness through productivity gains from innovation and better client relationships. These productivity gains stem from access to a broader range of talent – knowledge, skills, abilities, experience, and aptitudes – from employing a wide range of workers[27,28]. This includes the contribution from employing older workers.

In Australia, both the equity and the diversity approaches are tinged by early assumptions about the model worker[29]. The 1907 *Harvester Case*[29] articulated the socio-legal position that wages should be set so that a worker, usually male, white, able-bodied, and working full-time, could provide the necessities for a home-based wife and family. This underlying model influenced the development of a workplace culture of an uninterrupted career and long hours[30,31]. Not only is this model of the worker no longer the reality for many people in the workforce – from single parents to working women to differently-abled employees – it also does not take into account the concept that someone may wish to, or may need to, keep working to an older age.

Older workers themselves may have preferred forms of work that differ from this narrow and simplistic model. Older workers with financial and family commitments seek employment that offers them job security and flexibility[32]. Prospective true retirees[33] are looking for non-permanent and flexible work options as they transition to retirement.

Older workers are not a static or homogenous group. Who is and is not an older worker changes over time and with the context, the political and social agenda, and the perspective of the one applying the term. There are telling community and commercial reasons to review and redress age-related barriers to employment and come to grips with faulty perceptions of older workers. Older workers themselves have a range of needs and aspirations related to their employment depending on their financial means, health concerns and psychological needs for finding meaning and identity through work. Established workplace practices and underlying workplace culture are misaligned with the reality for older workers.

In stereotyping, once we make an assumption, we tend to stick with it.

TWO

Looking through Age-tinted Glasses

Exploring Negative and Positive Perceptions of Older Workers

Age discrimination occurs where someone is treated less favourably in comparison to others on the basis of their age (*Age Discrimination Act 2004* (Cwlth) s 14)[1]. Despite more than a decade of protection as a result of age discrimination legislation, the imperative of the equity agenda, and the strength of the business case favouring diversity in the workplace, many employers still mirror society in terms of holding negative stereotypes of older workers.

Stereotypes can be valuable. We use stereotypes to help speed up human processing by reducing the large amount of environmental information about others to known, general categories. We can hold both cultural and personal stereotypes. So instead of dealing with the world with no quick and simple way to interpret what we experience, we use stereotyping to help us manage 'processing overload' by generalising from beliefs about a class or group to the individual in front of us[2].

While stereotypes are useful tools, stereotyping can become problematic. When stereotypes are overused we no longer see the way in which an individual may differ from our personal or cultural perceptions of the group to which they may belong. In stereotyping, it may not even matter if the individual actually belongs to the group to which we have assigned them – once we make an assumption, we tend to stick with it. So we continue to apply stereo-types to a person or a group even when the stereotype no longer represents reality[3]. It is these negative stereotypes and misperceptions that actively create barriers to employment for older workers.

Negative views about older workers

Labour market trends and new technologies require workers with capabilities to learn new skills, unlearn irrelevant skills, and keep up-to-date with changes in technology, legislation, and regulation[4,5,6]. Unfortunately, as across our wider society, employers assume that older workers have out-dated skills and have difficulty learning new skills[7,8], and that they are resistant to change[9,10]. Employers further believe that older workers are more costly to employ and that there is little prospect of obtaining a return on the investment in training for older workers[8,11,12], because older workers have difficulty taking-on new learning and, anyway, may not continue to work for very long. Employers hold views that older workers lack drive and energy[13], have poor inter-personal behaviours[14,16], and poor health[8,15]. Consequently, older workers are seen as unproductive.

If employers do not believe they will get a return on their training investment in older workers, then they are unlikely to provide training for those older workers and could even discourage older workers from seeking or participating in training programs. Older workers may therefore have outdated skills and be less productive. In such a negative organisational context, older workers could be reluctant to train their replacements in their tacit skills and knowledge that they have accumulated over a working life[13]. They may feel bitter, upset, confused and humiliated, which can in turn influence older workers' ill health and depression[14,16]. The potential for self-fulfilling prophecy is evident.

Positive views about older workers

Not all perceptions of older workers are negative. Employers hold positive views of older workers as well.

Older workers are seen as having valuable task skills, as well as knowledge and skills that are specific to, and important for, the organisation[13,17]. Such skills can be tacit – that is, knowledge and abilities that are acquired through practice and experience[18]. These useful skills can also represent organisational citizenship behaviours which are supportive and voluntary extra-role behaviours[19] and membership behaviours, which are related to joining and staying with an organisation[20].

Employers view older workers as having valuable attributes such as low absenteeism[21], non-disruptive work behaviours[22], loyalty and low turnover, a strong work ethic, and reliability and punctuality[13]. However, these positive attributes can be linked more to older workers' tacit skills and knowledge, membership behaviours and organisation citizenship behaviours.

In contemporary organisations and in the emerging workplace, employers want and seek flexible non-task-specific skills in new employees[13]. While the tacit skills and knowledge, good membership behaviours and organisation citizenship behaviours of older workers are valued by the current employer, these skills and background are less attractive to a new employer that may require very different specific skills[13]. Older workers' in-depth organisation-specific knowledge often lacks transferability to other organisations and industries, which in turn limits the market value of those skills and knowledge[13,23,24]. Older workers' loyalty and tenure can translate to the stagnation of an organisation's succession pipelines[25] and may signal out-of-date skills. It seems that even older workers' 'past training, qualifications and experience' (*Age Discrimination Act 2004* (Cwlth) s 18)[1] – valuable attributes that should help sustain employment – can instead create barriers to ongoing employment.

Employers and the community as a whole hold mixed views of their older workers. Negative perceptions of older workers suggest reduced performance due to non-current skills and poor health. Further, perceptions that older workers have difficulty learning, resist change and will not provide a return on investment in training, makes them seem less valuable to their current employer and less attractive to prospective employers. So-called positive views of older workers' good behaviours do not sufficiently counter these negative perceptions. While strong job- and organisation-specific skills and compliant work membership behaviours are valued, they are seen as less transferrable and less marketable.

Takeaways

Employers hold negative stereotypes that older workers are more costly than younger workers, have poorer health and declining physical and mental abilities, are poorly skilled, and resist learning.

Older workers have valuable organisation and job-related knowledge, life experience, work ethic, commitment, and learning ability.

Overt age-related stereotypes
can be challenged.
Subtle cues
are more difficult to address.

THREE

What's Real, What's Not?

Challenging Employment Barriers for Older Workers

Significant and established negative perceptions of older workers create barriers to the ability of older workers to gain and sustain employment and to further develop their careers. Although employers value some of the attributes they perceive in older workers, employers still tend to prefer hiring younger workers. So, do employers' negative views actually reflect the reality of older workers? Are older workers less productive? Are older workers relatively more costly, poorly skilled, and burdened with declining health and physical and mental abilities? Don't older workers' positive attributes and good work behaviours balance out the supposed performance deficits? What is real, and what's not in our perceptions of older workers at work? The research suggests that the negative stereotypes do not always reflect reality, especially in considering any particular older worker.

Cost of older workers

Employers perceive that younger workers have lower wages, more current skills, and a longer potential tenure for a better return on investment in training. Historically, older workers have had an expectation of a pay premium for their experience and tacit skills[1,2,3] and workers generally felt that older workers were legitimately due a return on their contribution across their working life in training their novice co-workers[4]. However, within the fluidity of the contemporary labour market, older workers' extensive task-specific and organisation-specific skills are less marketable, and age and long experience are no longer requirements for many senior/supervisory positions[1,4]. These days, markets provide less justification for substantial age or experience-based pay differentials.

Where older workers do receive a pay premium, employers can reduce overall wages by preferentially targeting older workers when restructuring and down-sizing. As part of these processes, employers may also encourage older workers to self-select out[2], for example with voluntary separation packages. Older workers are removed or leave even at the employer's risk of losing organisational knowledge.

Older workers have different preferences for the type of work that they need and want to do, depending on their circumstances[5]. Not all older workers are ready to, willing to or able to retire or simply down-shift into lower-level, lower paid or part-time work. With financial and psychological needs[1] to continue in employment, older workers who prematurely leave the workforce, are thrust back into the labour market. The employment arrangements in the new job, however, may end up being at a lower rate of pay and often peripheral and precarious – that is, less valued non-core jobs and less stable contingent work, such as casual, seasonal or relief work. There can be an advantage for organisations in older workers taking on these less favourable employment arrangements. Lower paid, contingent employees provide numerical flexibility[1,4,6,7] enabling organisations to seamlessly ramp-up their workforce and down-size as needed. With these advantages, employers may be less motivated to challenge such convenient negative perceptions of older workers.

In 2014, the ABS recorded that, rather than older workers being more costly, their average weekly earnings actually declined after age forty-five[8]. In Australia, maximum earnings occurred during the prime age – between twenty-five and fifty-four years[9]. Older workers earned between 9 per cent and 14 per cent less than prime age workers.

Several possible explanations exist for the earnings differential between those under fifty-five years and those over fifty-five. Older workers had relatively poorer education levels[10] which influenced their earning potential. Older workers sought part-time work to manage their own health needs or to meet the demand to provide care for others. Older workers may also have been pressured into early/ phased retirement or to take lower paid jobs[7,11].

The negative perception that older workers are relatively more costly to employ was not evident in older workers' recorded earnings. This may be a reflection of older workers actively seeking their preferred work arrangement and employers structuring their workplaces for numerical flexibility. However, as the better-educated, under fifty-four-year-old, prime age workers become older workers, their average earnings are likely to increase to match the market. Better educated workers earn more and are better able to sustain ongoing employment.

Skills of older workers

Older workers may not have had access to the training they need in order to keep their skills current. This may be due to negative stereotypes about their ability to learn or because employers could not calculate an acceptable return on the training investment.

Around 25 per cent of workers who are fifty-five or older feel that they are subjected to age-related discrimination in employment[12], and between 15 per cent and 25 per cent believe they have experienced age discrimination, particularly, in job application processes[13]. Even when matched on gender, education, and work experience, older job applicants have a lower chance of being selected for a job than younger applicants[3]. Whether apparent or real, non-selection of older workers for recruitment, development and promotion may be explained in terms of older workers' non-current skills, their lack of recent training, and due to in-group/out-group perceptions of skill levels.

Skills can deteriorate over time or lose their value as job requirements change[14]. Older workers use technology less than younger people and are minimally involved in formal education. Older workers report a 9 per cent decrease in computer use/skill compared to prime age workers[15] and a decreased rate of technology uptake. Among fifty-five to sixty-four year olds, 79 per cent use the internet at home compared to around 95 per cent of those under fifty-five years of age. People aged forty-five years to sixty-five or older had the lowest average number of hours spent online at home per week[16]. Older workers have minimal engagement in formal education: up to 5 per cent of forty-five to sixty-four year olds are engaged in formal education compared to 10 per cent to 15 per cent for those aged between twenty-five and forty-four years[17]. Older workers themselves may not recognise or accept that their skills are no longer current or that their skillsets are less valuable in the job market and less critical for employers.

Social identity theory[18] suggests that there is a tendency for people to rate the skills of their identified in-group more highly[1] than the skills of out-groups. For older workers, this means that a bias towards their in-group based around age could blind them to the need to develop their skills [7]. Older workers may have failed to take opportunities to update their skills[19] and may believe that their experience exempts them from training[20] or that they learn more effectively on the job[21].

Training outcomes for older workers are also influenced by the trainer's negative perceptions of older workers' ability to learn. These negative stereotypes dominate even when trainers have some positive views of older worker trainees, such as older workers' strong work ethic[22]. Older workers therefore may have low expectations that enhancing their skills through training will actually lead to benefits or rewards[14].

While the education and skills levels of older workers are used to demonstrate that they may not meet employer expectations, older workers can take action to position themselves more favourably in the labour market. For example, in recruitment processes, older workers can compensate for any negative perceptions with evidence of relevant work experience, recent training, and the correct level of education for the particular job vacancy[3]. While avoiding the convenience of blaming the victim, it is naïve to ignore older workers' behaviours, preferences, and circumstances that limit their skills development and currency and reduce their job marketability.

Health and abilities of older workers

Negative stereotypes suggest that older workers are less productive due to their poor health and declining physical and mental abilities. There is a gradual decline across the body's systems over the human lifecycle. For example, the brain size of younger adults decreases at 0.12 per cent per year while for those over 52 years the rate of decrease is 0.35 per cent[23]. However, in 2012, the Australian Active Ageing Survey[24] reported that 80 per cent of people over fifty years of age responded that they were happy and healthy. There are comparatively few people between fifty and sixty-four years in nursing homes in Australia. In 2010 – 2011, 2601 people aged fifty to fifty-nine years and 3161 people aged sixty to sixty-four years were in nursing home accommodation, against 22 737 people between sixty-five and seventy-four years and 56821 people between seventy-five and eighty-four years in nursing home accommodation[25]. For those between sixty-five and seventy-four years, 98.3 per cent lived in private dwellings[25]. As we age, the impact of the decline in the body's systems varies across individuals, and most people learn to effectively compensate for any decline[24].

Older workers' workforce participation rate is 35 per cent, yet older workers represent 7 per cent of work-related injuries and illnesses, 19 per cent of serious workers compensation claims and 35 per cent of work fatalities[26]. Workers over forty-five years of age account for almost half of all injuries/illnesses, serious workers' compensation claims and fatalities[26]. Historically, older male workers have more unavoidable absences due to longer recovery times[27]. This raises the question of whether older workers are over-represented in injury and illness, or if ill and injured older workers are under-supported in utilising safe work practices and in their return to work following illness and injury.

Ageing has differential effects on cognition, with areas of potential improvement with age and areas of comparative deficit. There may be age-related deficits in working memory and processing speed which are related to a decline in spatial ability and reasoning ability[28]. Objective health measures, such as lung function and blood pressure, show impacts on memory, processing speed, visuospatial ability, multi-tasking and reasoning that start to degrade from early adulthood[29,30]. However, other forms of reasoning, such as verbal reasoning, and memory for content knowledge – that is, knowledge and experience that people have learned, such as general world knowledge and verbal and numerical skills – can be maintained and may improve as we age[23,29,30,31].

Normal ageing impacts cognition and memory – and memory deficits can occur at any time during the life-cycle from injury, illness or substance abuse[24] – but reported age-related differences in cognitive ability may also be due to individual differences and a range of other factors[29,32]. Harris (1990)[31] suggested that early ageing studies focused on the elderly in institutions overlooking fitter and healthier older people in the general population, giving the impression that most of the ageing were, in fact, ill. Jeske and Stamov Roßnagel's (2015)[33] literature review suggested that established laboratory testing of cognitive skill focused on maximal performance – that is, under memory load and time pressure and with low work task relevance – rather than on tasks and the proficient performance that is expected in the usual course of the work day. Furthermore, these assessments removed some factors that strengthen performance at work, such as self-regulation, expertise, motivation, prior knowledge and strategies that older workers routinely utilise in their work performance[33]. Workers could be reprimanded for failing to apply these traits, skills and strategies in their work.

Individual differences across older workers also contribute to age-related differences in mental abilities. Cardio-vascular fitness and physical capability influence cognitive ability[32] and levels of physical well-being may account for some differences in mental abilities and performance of older workers. Lower levels of education are related to more rapid decreases in memory performance and retention of learned knowledge and skills[29]. Practice can compensate for age-related reduction in motor skills and task performance[34, 35], and higher education, lower blood pressure and good health may protect against cognitive decline[29]. For most healthy older people, cognitive decline is gradual and negligible until the late seventies, and possibly beyond that[24,36,37].

Organisational context[38] and individual responses to stereotype threat[39] also impact reported cognitive performance. Organisations can create, at times inadvertently, an organisational context that calls-up negative stereotypes of older workers. Workforce descriptors such as *'aspiring'* and *'eager to learn'*, suggest a youth-oriented context[38]. Work cultures may embed long-held and still popular expressions that can limit older workers' confidence[40]: we continue to hear about the problem of old dogs in relation to new tricks. Promoting a non-inclusive context increases the salience of in-group/out-group membership. When older workers identify with the threatened age out-group[39] – especially when they do not feel comfortable or happy being part of the older worker group[41] – and a negative stereotype is invoked[38], older workers report lower levels of job satisfaction and engagement[42], and experience diminished memory performance in cognitive tests[39]. A more inclusive work context that promotes a broader range of contributors to organisational effectiveness may provide an uplift in overall staff performance, including that of older workers.

Older workers and age discrimination

Across the labour market, workers believe that at times they have been unfairly discriminated against in employment for a variety of reasons. Seven to eight per cent of all workers believe they have been discriminated against in employment – predominantly on the basis of age[13]. Perceptions of age discrimination increase with the age of the job applicant[12]. Around 25 per cent of workers who are fifty-five years or older are conscious of age discrimination, for example, when applying for a job, contrasting with 9 per cent of those under forty-four years and around 15 per cent of workers between forty-five and fifty-four years[13].

Older workers perceive age discrimination in the organisational context. The organisation context includes the processes to apply for a job, to appoint to a position and for promotion, and the business processes to identify employees for voluntary separation and select employees for involuntary termination, such as when down-sizing [43,44]. This context provides cues that, on the basis of their age, older workers are less valued by the organisation than younger workers[38].

Negative age stereotypes can influence the behaviour and performance of older workers, which further embeds those same negative perceptions. In a negative organisational context, older workers may lack the confidence to take-on learning and development challenges[45] and may have poorer memory performance[46]. Negative stereotypes can also affect older workers when they identify as members of the out-group, which can then adversely impact interview behaviours and on-the-job performance[38,42]. Poorer cognitive functioning, reduced willingness to take on challenges and pursue new learning, and less polished interview techniques all serve as evidence to prop-up the non-appointment of older workers and support decisions that lead to the preferential exit of older workers from employment[44].

Proponents of social identity theory suggest that since older hiring managers tend to recruit older workers and Australia's working population is ageing, then over time employers will come to recognise the value of older workers. An alternate view is that the scarcity of youth resources may make younger workers an even more prized option[3,4,47].

Perceptions of a negative influence of mature age on employment prospects have changed. In the ABS 2014–2015 data[48], 17 per cent of workers who were fifty-five years or older reported that they felt they would be considered to be too old by a prospective employer; a figure which was down from 21 per cent in 2013 and 30 per cent in 2005. This change may have arisen due to shortages of critical skills and predicted substantial losses of staff to the global economy and from the increasing ageing population which, in turn, have forced employers to explore all categories of workers, even peripheral and less preferred workers[49,50]. It remains to be seen if the forecast increased participation of older workers represents a real change in organisations' perceptions of older workers and if older workers are disproportionately affected by economic bounty and strife.

Older workers' with low levels of satisfaction and low job quality attribute this to age discrimination[13]. However, it is also likely that a discriminatory organisational context produces low job quality and low worker satisfaction. More promisingly, older workers with good job search skills, and older workers with a consistent work history, perceive fewer age-related barriers to employment[12,51]. Those workers who have successfully maintained their employability past seventy-five years of age have above-average qualifications, a history of accomplishment, an established professional reputation and networks, specialist and in-demand skillsets, and above-average good health[52]. However, Patrickson (2016)[52] noted that more typical older job seekers are unlikely to have the particular traits, abilities and skills to enable them to compete as effectively with younger workers.

Overt age-related stereotypes can be challenged. Subtle organisational context cues are more difficult to address both for older workers and for organisations trying to manage their diversity.

Takeaway

Negative stereotypes do not always reflect reality, especially in considering any particular older worker, and a non-inclusive organisational context can adversely impact the performance of older workers.

Notes

An inclusive organisational context
supports employees
across the whole working lifecycle.

FOUR

Our People, Our Greatest Asset

Leading and Managing Older Workers

Employers and prospective employers of older workers can take steps to overcome age-related barriers to employment in an effort to recruit and retain older workers. To attract, retain and capitalise on the knowledge and experience of older workers, organisations need an inclusive organisational context that reduces stereotype threat, supportive work practices, to encourage lifelong learning, and to train managers to effectively lead and manage older workers.

An inclusive organisational context goes beyond the fabric of the workplace and programs such as flexible work practices, to challenge the implicit actions in an organisation that demonstrate how – or if – older workers are valued[1,2]. An organisation's implicit beliefs about older workers are often showcased in recruitment advertising. Images of younger workers with catch-phrases such as *'dynamic workplace'* and *'developing team'* signal that older workers are not the target of the recruitment advertisement or that they may not feel a part of the working environment[3,4]. Where stereotype threat is invoked, de-motivated and uncertain older workers may avoid challenging assignments that could otherwise be opportunities to demonstrate their value[5]. In an organisational context where negative stereotypes are not activated and age anxiety is not so readily invoked, older workers' performance should more accurately reflect their actual abilities[6,7].

Organisations can design work practices to support employees across their whole working lifecycle. However, older workers tend to baulk at special age-related programs, because they perceive that these programs embed negative perceptions rather than support their needs. Work practices are more effective when they are designed and intended for all workers and accessible to the range of workers[8]. These work practices should still accommodate older workers' particular circumstances of increased caring responsibilities[9], altered capacity to meet job demands of heavy physical work and shift work[9], and the financial necessity to continue working.

Appropriate age-friendly practices can be implemented that value older workers. Such practices include job redesign to reduce physicality while still maintaining worker status[4]; flexible work arrangements to support child and elder caring responsibilities (which may also have wider workforce appeal[10]); work-retirement transitions[11]; recognition programs that respect and reward the in-demand skills and experience that older workers possess[12,13]; opportunities for cross-mentoring; and actions to improve older worker job satisfaction through managing work intensification[9,14].

Employers can encourage lifelong learning across the careers of all employees. Employers should both encourage older workers in their learning and development[15] and expect older workers to keep their skillset current and to learn new in-demand skills[13]. Furthermore, organisations can educate and inform trainers to recognise and overcome their own negative stereotypes about older-aged trainees to ensure optimal training outcomes for all learners[16]. Older workers also need to develop behaviours that are better suited to contemporary workplaces, such as responsibility for their own skills development and proactivity in career planning[17]. Where employers hold workers to the same standard of participation in development, older workers will have less latitude to avoid actively participating in the learning experience. Importantly, older workers will have better access to training, thereby increasing their likelihood of continuous work by assuring their productivity and demonstrating a return on the training investment.

Organisations may also provide tailored development for managers (including younger managers) in leading and managing older workers. Managers can be trained to reduce the impacts of negative stereotypes and in-group/out-group formation on overall productivity levels and to recognise more similarities than differences between age-groups[18]. Employers can train managers to communicate with older workers to uncover issues that prompt older workers to make the decision to retire or change jobs[14]. Older workers often start thinking about retirement or a job change-down after a personal health shock, when they are no longer able to manage the work intensity or physical demands of the job, or as their family caring responsibilities multiply. Employers are at risk of losing older workers prematurely, often to financially insecure retirement or less satisfying and lower paid part-time jobs or contingent work. Informed managers can work together with their older workers to rebalance these emerging issues in the workplace.

Action Points

- Develop an inclusive organisational context that does not create or contribute to anxiety about age

- Provide supportive work practices for all workers that encompass age-friendly practices

- Encourage and support lifelong learning and expect skills to be kept current

- Train managers to effectively lead and manage older workers

Takeaway

Inclusive and flexible working practices, and targeted manager training can retain productive older workers in the workforce.

Older workers can balance their past experience with openness to change.

FIVE

Hints for Older Workers

Walking Through a Few Strategies

Organisations and society as a whole may someday come to recognise the benefits of better utilisation of older workers, particularly as the median age of the working population shifts upwards. In the meantime, older workers can take steps to improve their own employment outcomes.

Older workers are more successful in their job seeking activities and more sustained in their employment when their skills, experience and education are well-matched to the requirements of the role, including the remuneration for the position. Organisations may not place a premium on additional experience where that experience does not directly advance the business objectives of the role. Budgets may also confine hiring decisions to value and compensate just those skills needed to get the job done. Older workers should match their salary expectations and costs of their training needs to the role requirements. Employers see little value in remunerating any worker, older workers included, to meet the worker's lifestyle commitments, upgrade out-of-date skills, or to compensate them for ancillary skills and experience.

Older workers may not have difficulty in learning new skills. However, older workers can be reluctant to risk learning failure and loss of prestige. Likewise, they have learning styles which have an impact on learning time (e.g., in self-paced online learning) or require different learning channels (e.g., opportunities for application and practice), or they may resist personal responsibility for job readiness. Older workers can design and implement their own life-long learning plan with learning goals to keep needed skills current, identify and learn valuable new skills, and participate in structured and on-the-job learning.

People's physical health and cognitive ability change throughout the course of their lifetime. Older workers, and workers in general, support their employability by maintaining good physical health with nutrition and exercise[1,2], and keeping intellectually active. Successful older workers have demonstrated the value of maintaining professional networks in contributing to their employability[3]. Furthermore, older workers may have a critical *'been there, done that'* approach which dampens other workers' enthusiasm for new ways of doing things, and may also seem unsupportive of management and organisational objectives. Older workers can strike a balance between relying on their past experiences and being open to change in the current situation.

Hints

- Match skills, experience, education and salary expectations to the requirements of the role

- Develop a lifelong learning plan

- Stay in good physical health and intellectually active

- Maintain professional, industry and social networks

- Bring experience and openness to change to the job

Takeaway

Older workers can sustain their employment through education, up-skilling, effective interpersonal skills, and being adaptable to change.

Notes

Recognise what is real about perceptions of older workers and let go of what is not.

Conclusion

We are all ageing all the time and ageing impacts all workers. As life expectancy increases and community and individual expectations rise about the real length of working life, age discrimination has the potential to affect us all. Workers are affected very personally through exclusion from income earning, promotion, training and career development. The nation as a whole will feel these effects, as reduced economic advantages of higher workforce participation narrows the base for government revenue and requires increased levels of government expenditure to support the growing ageing population.

The equity approach to disadvantage seeks to promote a fair share of the benefits of employment by removing barriers to historically employment-disadvantaged groups such as older workers. The business case for managing diversity recognises the contribution to organisational effectiveness that a diverse workforce offers, including capitalising on older workers' attributes and abilities. However, persistent negative stereotypes that older workers are more costly, less productive, have declining abilities and are difficult to supervise due to poor interpersonal behaviours, raise barriers to their ongoing employment. In addition, an organisational context that implicitly devalues older workers and triggers these stereotypes can actually promote negative performance and skill deficits among older workers. In some respects, older workers may also confirm, contribute to and collude with these negative stereotypes. While employers may recognise the business case for diversity and the value of older workers, older workers need to be willing to take action themselves to realise the benefits they can offer in the workplace.

Organisations and older workers alike have a role to play in addressing employment-related barriers. Both employers and workers can help to create an inclusive organisational context by encouraging and participating in lifelong learning, and developing managers to support a diverse workforce. With decreasing workforce proportions of younger workers, employers' penchant for the *bright and shiny* needs to undergo a change. Older workers may not be exuberant about organisational life, but their inconvenient questions can highlight pitfalls, and with their strong work ethic and commitment, they will be in a good position to offer valuable solutions.

When grappling with the complex issues of employment barriers for older workers, it is tempting to point to the *other* as the cause, whether that is age or age discrimination. However, organisations, employers and older workers can all benefit from exploring their perceptions of older workers. Older workers, like all workers and all human beings, are not perfect – every stage of life has its developmental challenges and learning opportunities. By recognising what is real about our perceptions of older workers and letting go of what is not, we promote more effective organisations and open ourselves to a richer life experience.

Age can be unlimited.

Notes

Appendix

TABLE 1 – Negative Views of Older Workers
Older workers are more costly to employ

Older workers:
   • Have more experience and qualifications than required for job vacancies
   • Have health issues and declining physicality that impacts their productivity
   • Are paid, or expect to be paid, highly relative to their productivity
   • Provide a poor return on investment in their training – they retire or reduce their working hours before the value of training is realised
   • Are poor learners so training takes longer and is more costly

Older workers are less productive
Older workers: • Do not want to or are unable to work full-time or a full work week • Do not want to work the long hours required to get the job done • Are no longer competent • Think slowly – they are not quick to pick-up things
Older workers do not keep their skills up-to-date
Older workers: • Have little interest in new skills or in their personal development • Have skills and qualifications that are not in-demand • Have task-specific skills and knowledge that are not transferrable to other jobs, employers or industries • Have difficulty learning new skills • Are untrainable – they are too set in their ways and resist change • Take longer to learn new technology and complex tasks

Older workers lack drive, ambition and energy
Older workers: • Are not enthusiastic or motivated to succeed • Are not innovative and do not wish to try new things • Have less development or promotion potential
Older workers resist change
Older workers: • Are not adaptable • Are averse to taking risks • Are closed to new ideas • Know the organisation's change history and so are less compliant with change processes
Older workers have poor health and are losing their faculties
Older workers: • Are not as fit and have more work injuries, and so are more often absent from work • Are losing their physical capability and mental abilities – they are forgetful and so less reliable

Older workers do not fit-in and are not good team players
Older workers: • Lack self-confidence and are shy, or they are over-bearing and presumptuous • Are negative, cynical and discontented • Cannot relate to younger people and do not like working for younger managers • Do not want to share their knowledge with less experienced workers • Are long-winded, unfocused, and talk about inappropriate personal matters

TABLE 2 – Positive Views of Older Workers
Older workers are 'good employees'
Older workers: • Are more reliable in attending work and have less absenteeism • Arrive on-time and keep good working hours • Keep in good health and do not report work-related accidents • Follow instructions – they do what they are asked to do • Manage their own behaviours • 'Work-in' with others and are not disruptive in the workplace

Older workers have valuable skills

Older workers:
    • Have job-specific skills that their employer values
    • Have critical skills and job knowledge that they can teach to others

Older workers are good organisational citizens

Older workers:
    • Are committed and stay for longer with the organisation
    • Are loyal and have a good work ethic
    • Are good decision-makers
    • Support their managers

References

Introduction

[1] Billett, S., Dymock, D., Johnson, G., and Martin, G. (2011). 'Overcoming the paradox of employers' views about older workers.' *The International Journal of Human Resource Management*, 22: 6, 1248–1261. doi:10.1080/09585192.201 1.559097

[2] Coupland, C., Tempest, S., and Barnatt, C. (2008). 'What are the implications of the new UK age discrimination legislation for research and practice?' *Human Resource Management Journal*, 18: 4, 423–431.

[3] Australian Bureau of Statistics. (2014). Deaths, Australia, 2014 (Catalogue No. 3302.0.). Retrieved from http://www.abs.gov.au/AUSSTATS/abs@.nsf/mf/3302.0 (accessed 23 July 2016).

Chapter 1

[1] Brough, P., Johnson, G., Drummond, S., Pennisi, S., and Timms, C. (2011). 'Comparisons of cognitive ability

and job attitudes of older and younger workers.' *Equality, Diversity and Inclusion: An International Journal*, 30: 2, 105–126. doi:10.1108/02610151111116508

[2] Appannah, A. and Biggs, S. (2015). 'Age-friendly organisations: The role of organisational culture and the participation of older workers.' *Journal of Social Work Practice*, 29: 1, 37–51.

[3] Australian Bureau of Statistics. (2016). Barriers and Incentives to Labour Force Participation, Australia, July 2014 to June 2015 (Catalogue No. 6239.0). Retrieved from http://www.abs.gov.au/ausstats/abs@. nsf/Latestproducts/6239.0Media%20Release1July%20 2014%20to%20June%202015?opendocument&tabname=S ummary&prodno=6239.0&issue=July%202014%20to%20 June%202015&num=&view= (accessed 23 July 2016).

[4] Australian Bureau of Statistics. (2013). Australian Labour Market Statistics, July 2013 (Catalogue No. 6105.0). Retrieved from http://www.abs.gov.au/AUSSTATS/abs@. nsf/Previousproducts/6105.0Feature%20Article2July%20 2013?opendocument&tabname=Summary&prodno=6105. 0&issue=July%202013&num=&view= (accessed 30 March 2016).

[5] Australian Bureau of Statistics. (2012). Disability and Labour Force Participation, 2012 (Catalogue No. 4433.0.55.006). Retrieved from http://www.abs.gov.au/ ausstats%5Cabs@.nsf/0/C7C72D7706E9BED0CA257D E2000BDC60?Opendocument (accessed 23 July 2016).

[6] *Fair Work Act 2009* (Cwlth) http://www.austlii.edu.au/

[7] Australian Government, Department of Human Services. (2016a). https://www.humanservices.gov.au/customer/ser- vices/centrelink/age-pension (accessed 10 July 2016).

[8] Australian Government, Department of Human Services. (2016b). https://www.humanservices.gov.au/organisations/about-us/budget/budget-2014-15/budget-measures/older-australians/increase-age-pension-qualifying-age-70-years (accessed 21 September 2017).

[9] Australian Human Rights Commission. (2013). Fact or fiction? Stereotypes of older Australians Research Report 2013. https://www.humanrights.gov.au/sites/default/files/document/publication/Fact%20or%20Fiction_2013_WebVersion_FINAL_0.pdf (accessed 30 March 2016).

[10] McKay, S. (1998) as cited in Kirton, G. and Greene, A. (2010). *The dynamics of managing diversity: A critical approach, Oxford: Elsevier.*

[11] Australian Bureau of Statistics. (2015). Australian Demographic Statistics, December 2015 (Catalogue No. 3101.0). Retrieved from http://www.abs.gov.au/ausstats/abs@.nsf/mf/3101.0 (accessed 23 July 2016).

[12] Australian Bureau of Statistics. (2015). Population by Age and Sex, Regions of Australia, 2014 (Catalogue No. 3235.0). Retrieved from http://www.abs.gov.au/ausstats/abs@.nsf/Latestproducts/3235.0Main%20Features102014?opendocument&tabname=Summary&prodno=3235.0&issue=2014&num=&view= (accessed 23 July 2016).

[13] Australian Bureau of Statistics. (2014). Deaths, Australia, 2014 (Catalogue No. 3302.0.). Retrieved from http://www.abs.gov.au/AUSSTATS/abs@.nsf/mf/3302.0 (accessed 23 July 2016).

[14] Australian Government, Australian Institute of Health and Welfare. (2016). http://www.aihw.gov.au/deaths/life-expectancy/ (accessed 9 August 2016).

[15] Australian Government. (2015). Intergenerational report: Australia in 2055 Executive Summary. http://www.treasury.gov.au/~/media/Treasury/Publications%20and%20Media/Publications/2015/2015%20Intergenerational%20Report/Downloads/PDF/02_Exec_summary.ashx (accessed 14 March 2016).

[16] Australian Bureau of Statistics. (2016). Labour force Australia, detailed (Catalogue No. 6291.0.55.001). Retrieved from http://www.abs.gov.au http://www.abs.gov.au/ausstats/abs@.nsf/mf/6202.0 (accessed 23 July 2016).

[17] Productivity Commission. (2013). *An ageing Australia: Preparing for the future. Productivity Commission research paper, Melbourne: Commonwealth of Australia.*

[18] Patrickson, M. and Ranzijn, R. (2004). 'Bounded choices in work and retirement in Australia.' *Employee Relations,* 26: 4, 422–432. doi:10.1108.014250410544515

[19] Ranzijn, R. (2004). 'Role ambiguity: Older workers in the demographic transition.' *Ageing International,* 29: 3, 281–308.

[20] Roberts, I. (2006). 'Taking age out of the workplace: Putting older workers back in?' *Work, Employment and Society,* 20: 1, 67–86. doi:10.1177/0950017006061274

[21] Johnson, G., Billett, S., Dymock, D., and Martin, G. (2013). 'The discursive (re)positioning of older workers in Australian recruitment policy reform: An exemplary analysis of written and visual narratives.' *Equality, Diversity and Inclusion: An International Journal,* 32: 1, 4–21. doi:10.1108/02610151311305588

[22] MacDermott, T. (2014). 'Older workers and extended workforce participation: Moving beyond the 'barriers to

work' approach.' *International Journal of Discrimination and the Law*, 14: 2, 83–98. doi:10.1177/1358229113520211

[23] *Anti-discrimination Act 1991* (Qld) http://www.austlii.edu.au/

[24] *Age Discrimination Act 2004* (Cwlth) http://www.austlii.edu.au/

[25] Acker, J. (2006). 'Inequality regimes: Gender, class, and race in organizations.' *Gender & Society*, 20: 4, 441–464. doi:10.1177/0891243206289499

[26] Australian Human Rights Commission. (2011). Legislation. https://www.humanrights.gov.au/our-work/legal/legislation (accessed 6 August 2016).

[27] Wrench, J. (2005). 'Diversity management can be bad for you.' *Race & Class*, 46: 3, 73–84. doi:10.1177/030696805050019

[28] O'Brien, K., Scheffer, M., van Nes, E., and van der Lee, R. (2015). 'How to break the cycle of low workforce diversity: A model for change.' *PLoS ONE*, 10: 7, 1–15. doi:10.1371/journal.pone.0133208

[29] *Ex parte H.V. McKay* [1907] 2 CAR 1.

[30] Wirth, L. (2001). *Breaking through the glass ceiling: Women in management. Geneva: International Labour Office.*

[31] Collinson, D. and Hearn, J. (1994) as cited in Kirton, G. and Greene, A. (2010). *The dynamics of managing diversity: A critical approach, Oxford: Elsevier.*

[32] Shomos, A., Turner, E., and Will, L. (2013). *Forms of work in Australia. Productivity Commission staff working paper. Melbourne: Commonwealth of Australia.*

[33] Perera, S., Sardeshmukh, K., and Kulik, C. (2015). 'In and out: Job exits of older workers.' *Asia Pacific Journal of Human Resources*, 53, 4–21. doi: 10.1111/1744-7941.12051

Chapter 2

[1] *Age Discrimination Act 2004* (Cwlth) http://www.austlii.edu.au/

[2] Cuddy, A. and Fiske, S. (2002). "Doddering but dear: Process, content and function in stereotyping of older persons", in Nelson, T. (Ed.), *Ageism: Stereotyping and prejudice against older persons*, MIT Press, Cambridge, MA, 1–26.

[3] Maurer, T., Barbiete, F., Weiss, E., and Lippstreu, M. (2008). 'New measures of stereotypical beliefs about older workers' ability and desire for development: Exploration among employees age 40 and over.' *Journal of Managerial Psychology*, 23, 395–418.

[4] Thite, M. (2004). 'Strategic positioning of HRM in knowledge-based organizations.' *The Learning Organization*, 11: 1, 28–44.

[5] Kelly, R. and Lewis, P. (2010). 'The change in labour skills in Australia over the business cycle.' *Australian Bulletin of Labour*, 36: 3, 260–277.

[6] Martin, G., Dymock, D., Billett, S., and Johnson, G. (2014). 'In the name of meritocracy: Managers' perceptions of policies and practices for training older workers.' *Ageing & Society*, 34, 992–1018. doi:10.1017/S0144686X12001432

[7] Coupland, C., Tempest, S., and Barnatt, C. (2008). 'What are the implications of the new UK age discrimination legislation for research and practice?' *Human Resource Management Journal*, 18: 4, 423–431.

[8] Nelson, T. (2016). 'The age of ageism.' *Journal of Social Issues*, 72: 1, 191–198. doi:10.1111.josi.12162

[9] MacDermott, T. (2014). 'Older workers and extended workforce participation: Moving beyond the 'barriers to work' approach.' *International Journal of Discrimination and the Law*, 14: 2, 83–98. doi:10.1177/1358229113520211

[10] Australian Human Rights Commission. (2015). National prevalence survey of age discrimination in the workplace. Author, Sydney.

[11] Heyma, A. and Nauta, A. (2014). 'What makes older job-seekers attractive to employers?' *De Economist*, 162, 397–414. doi:10.1007/s10645-014-9239-3

[12] Australian Human Rights Commission. (2008). Mature workers mean business. https://www.humanrights.gov.au/our-work/age-discrimination/publications/mature-workers-mean-business-2008 (accessed 19 June 2016).

[13] Ranzijn, R. (2004). 'Role ambiguity: Older workers in the demographic transition.' *Ageing International*, 29: 3, 281–308.

[14] Kulik, C. (2014). 'Spotlight on the context: How a stereotype threat framework might help organizations to attract and retain older workers.' *Industrial and Organizational Psychology*, 7: 3, 456–461.

[15] Billett, S., Dymock, D., Johnson, G., and Martin, G. (2011). 'Overcoming the paradox of employers' views about older workers.' *The International Journal of Human Resource Management*, 22: 6, 1248–1261. doi:10.1080/09585192.201 1.559097

[16] Cheung, C., Kam, P., and Ngan, R. (2011). 'Age discrimination in the labour market from the perspectives of

employers and older workers.' *International Social Work*, 54: 1, 118–136. doi:10.1177/0020872810372368

[17] Bittman, M., Flick, M., and Rice, J. (2001). *The recruitment of older Australian workers: A survey of employers in a high growth industry.* SPRC Report 6/01 Social Policy Research Centre University of New South Wales, Sydney.

[18] Myers, G. and Davids, K. (1992) as cited in Hunter Powell, P. and Watson, D. (2006). Service unseen: The hotel room attendant at work. *Hospitality Management* 25: 297–312. doi:10.1016/j.ijhm.2005.04.003

[19] Organ, D. W. (1997) as cited in Buller, P. F. and McEvoy, G. M. (2012). Strategy, human resource management and performance: Sharpening line of sight. *Human Resource Management Review*, 22: 43–56. doi:10.1016/j.hrmr.2011.11.002

[20] Shields, J. (2007). *Managing employee performance and reward: Concepts, practices, strategies. Melbourne, Victoria: Cambridge University Press.*

[21] Brough, P., Johnson, G., Drummond, S., Pennisi, S., and Timms, C. (2011). 'Comparisons of cognitive ability and job attitudes of older and younger workers.' *Equality, Diversity and Inclusion: An International Journal*, 30: 2, 105–126. doi:10.1108/02610151111116508

[22] Ng, T. and Feldman, D. (2008). 'The relationship of age to ten dimensions of job performance.' *Journal of Applied Psychology*, 93: 2, 392–423. doi: 10.1037/0021-9010.93.2.392

[23] Austin, M. and Droussitis, A. (2004) as cited in Wood, G., Wilkinson, A., and Harcourt, M. (2008). 'Age discrimination and working life: Perspectives and contestations – a review of the contemporary literature.' *International Journal of Management Reviews*, 10: 4, 425–442.

[24] Soldan, Z. and Nankervis, A. (2014). 'Employee perceptions of the effectiveness of diversity management in the Australian public service: Rhetoric and reality.' *Public Personnel Management*, 43: 4, 543. doi: 10.1177/0091026014533093

[25] Hornstein, Z., Gunderson, S., and Neumark, D. (2001) as cited in Wood, G., Wilkinson, A., and Harcourt, M. (2008). 'Age discrimination and working life: Perspectives and contestations – a review of the contemporary literature.' *International Journal of Management Reviews*, 10: 4, 425–442.

Chapter 3

[1] Ranzijn, R. (2004). 'Role ambiguity: Older workers in the demographic transition.' *Ageing International*, 29: 3, 281–308.

[2] Harcourt, M., Wilkinson, A., and Wood, G. (2010). 'The effects of anti-age discrimination legislation: A comparative analysis.' *The International Journal of Comparative Labour Law and Industrial Relations*, 26: 4, 447–465.

[3] Heyma, A. and Nauta, A. (2014). 'What makes older job-seekers attractive to employers?' *De Economist*, 162, 397–414. doi:10.1007/s10645-014-9239-3

[4] Roberts, I. (2006). 'Taking age out of the workplace: Putting older workers back in?' *Work, Employment and Society*, 20: 1, 67–86. doi:10.1177/0950017006061274

[5] Shomos, A., Turner, E., and Will, L. (2013). *Forms of work in Australia. Productivity Commission staff working paper. Melbourne: Commonwealth of Australia.*

[6] Coupland, C., Tempest, S., and Barnatt, C. (2008). 'What are the implications of the new UK age discrimination legislation for research and practice?' *Human Resource Management Journal*, 18: 4, 423–431.

[7] Wood, G., Wilkinson, A., and Harcourt, M. (2008). 'Age discrimination and working life: Perspectives and contestations – a review of the contemporary literature.' *International Journal of Management Reviews*, 10: 4, 425–442.

[8] Australian Bureau of Statistics. (2014). Characteristics of Employment, Australia, August 2014 (Catalogue No. 6333.0). Retrieved from http://www.abs.gov.au/ausstats/abs@.nsf/Latestproducts/6333.0Main%20Features1August%202014?opendocument&tabname=Summary&prodno=6333.0&issue=August%202014&num=&view= (accessed 30 March 2016).

[9] Australian Bureau of Statistics. (2013). Australian Labour Market Statistics, July 2013 (Catalogue No. 6105.0). Retrieved from http://www.abs.gov.au/AUSSTATS/abs@.nsf/Previousproducts/6105.0Feature%20Article2July%202013?opendocument&tabname=Summary&prodno=6105.0&issue=July%202013&num=&view= (accessed 30 March 2016).

[10] Productivity Commission. (2013). *An ageing Australia: Preparing for the future. Productivity Commission research paper, Melbourne: Commonwealth of Australia.*

[11] Hennekam, S. and Herrbach, O. (2015). The influence of age-awareness versus general HRM practices on the retirement decision of older workers. *Personnel Review*, 44: 1, 3–21. DOI 10.1108/PR-01-2014-0031

[12] Lyons, B., Wessel, J., Tai, Y., and Ryan, A. (2014). 'Strategies of job seekers related to age-related stereotypes.'

Journal of Managerial Psychology, 29: 8, 1009–1027. doi:10.1108/JMP-03-2013-0078

[13] Hahn, M. and Wilkins, R. (2013). 'Perceived job discrimination in Australia: Its correlates and consequences.' *Australian Journal of Labour Economics*, 16: 1, 43–64.

[14] Fossum, J. A., Paradise, R. D., and Robbins, N. E. (1986) as cited in Kooij, D., de Lange, A., Jansen, P., and Dikkers, J. (2007). 'Older workers motivation to continue to work: Five meanings of age. A conceptual view.' *Journal of Managerial Psychology*, 23: 4, 364–394.

[15] Chesters, J., Ryan, C., and Sinning, M. (2013). *Older Australians and the take-up of new technologies*. National Vocational Education and Training Research Program Ltd, Adelaide, South Australia.

[16] Australian Bureau of Statistics. (2014). Household use of information technology, Australia, 2014-15 (Catalogue No. 8146.0). Retrieved from http://www.abs.gov.au/ausstats/abs@.nsf/mf/8146.0 (accessed 23 July 2016).

[17] Australian Bureau of Statistics. (2015). Education and work, Australia, May 2015 (Catalogue No. 6227.0). Retrieved from http://www.abs.gov.au/ausstats/abs@.nsf/mf/6227.0 (accessed 23 July 2016).

[18] Tajfel, H. and Turner, J. C. (1986) as cited in Brough, P., Johnson, G., Drummond, S., Pennisi, S., and Timms, C. (2011). 'Comparisons of cognitive ability and job attitudes of older and younger workers.' *Equality, Diversity and Inclusion: An International Journal*, 30: 2, 105–126. doi:10.1108/02610151111116508

[19] Kooij, D., de Lange, A., Jansen, P., and Dikkers, J. (2007). 'Older workers motivation to continue to work: Five

meanings of age. A conceptual view.' *Journal of Managerial Psychology*, 23: 4, 364–394.

[20] Martin, G., Dymock, D., Billett, S., and Johnson, G. (2014). 'In the name of meritocracy: Managers' perceptions of policies and practices for training older workers.' *Ageing & Society*, 34, 992–1018. doi:10.1017/S0144686X12001432

[21] Warhurst, R. and Black, K. (2015). 'It's never too late to learn.' *Journal of Workplace Learning*, 27: 6, 457–472. doi: 10.1108/JWL-07-2014-0050

[22] McCausland, T., King, E., Bartholomew, L., Feyre, R., Ahmad, A., and Finkelstein, L. (2015). The technological age: The effects of perceived age in technology training. *Journal of Business and Psychology*, 30, 693–708. DOI 10.1007/s10869-014-9390-5

[23] APS Institute. (n.d.). *Practice certificate in services for older adults. Part 2: Neuropsychological aspects of ageing.* Accessed 10 January, 2018. http://elearning.psychology.org.au/course/view.php?id=38

[24] Queensland Government. Department of Communities, Child Safety and Disability Services. (2012). *Aging: Myth and reality.*

[25] Australian Bureau of Statistics. (2013). Where and how do Australia's older people live: Reflecting a nation: Stories from the 2011 census, 2012–2013 (Catalogue No. 2071.0). Retrieved fromhttp://www.abs.gov.au/ausstats/abs@.nsf/previousproducts/2071.0main%20features602012–2013?opendocument&tabname=summary&prodno=2071.0&issue=2012–2013&num=&view= (accessed 27 January 2018).

[26] Safe Work Australia. (2015). *Key work health and safety statistics, Australia, 2015, Canberra.*

[27] Rhodes, S. R. (1983) as cited in Bennington, L. and Tharenou, P. (1996). 'Older workers: Myths, evidence and implications for Australian managers.' *Asia Pacific Journal of Human Resources*, 34: 3, 63–76.

[28] Westerman, S. J., Davies, D. R., Glendon, A. I., and Stammers, R. B. (1998). Ageing and word processing competence: Compensation or compilation? *British Journal of Psychology*, 89, 579–597.

[29] Christensen, H. (2001). 'What cognitive changes can be expected with normal ageing?' *Australian and New Zealand Journal of Psychiatry*, 35, 768–775. doi: 10.1046/j.1440-1614.2001.00966.x

[30] Wardill, T. (2003) as cited in APS Institute. *Practice certificate in services for older adults. Part 1: Introduction to ageing.* Accessed 25 November, 2017. http://elearning.psychology.org.au/mod/book/view.php?id=1809&chapterid=1617

[31] Harris, D. (1990) as cited in Kossen, C. and Pedersen, C. (2008). Older workers in Australia: The myths, the realities and the battle over workforce flexibility. *Journal of Management & Organization*, 14: 1, 73–84.

[32] Brough, P., Johnson, G., Drummond, S., Pennisi, S., and Timms, C. (2011). 'Comparisons of cognitive ability and job attitudes of older and younger workers.' *Equality, Diversity and Inclusion: An International Journal*, 30: 2, 105–126. doi:10.1108/02610151111116508

[33] Jeske, D. and Stamov Roßnagel, C. (2015). Learning capability and performance in later working life: Towards a contextual view. *Education + Training*, 57, 378–391. DOI 10.1108/ET-08-2013-0107

[34] Bosman, E. A. (1993) as cited in Bennington, L. and Tharenou, P. (1996). Older workers: Myths, evidence and

implications for Australian managers. *Asia Pacific Journal of Human Resources*, 34: 3, 63–76.

[35] Luszcz, M. and Hinton, M. (1993) as cited in Bennington, L. and Tharenou, P. (1996). Older workers: Myths, evidence and implications for Australian managers. *Asia Pacific Journal of Human Resources*, 34: 3, 63–76.

[36] Hendricks, J. and Hendricks, C. D. (1977) as cited in Kossen, C. and Pedersen, C. (2008). Older workers in Australia: The myths, the realities and the battle over workforce flexibility. *Journal of Management & Organization*, 14: 1, 73–84.

[37] Hooyman, N. and Asuman-Kiyak, H. (1993) as cited in Kossen, C. and Pedersen, C. (2008). Older workers in Australia: The myths, the realities and the battle over workforce flexibility. *Journal of Management & Organization*, 14: 1, 73–84.

[38] Kulik, C. (2014). 'Spotlight on the context: How a stereotype threat framework might help organizations to attract and retain older workers.' *Industrial and Organizational Psychology*, 7: 3, 456–461.

[39] Hess, T. and Hinson, J. (2006). 'Age-related variation in the influences of aging stereotypes on memory in adulthood.' *Psychology and Aging*, 21: 3, 621–625. doi:10.1037/0882-797421.3.621

[40] Estes, C. and Binney, E. (1991) as cited in Kossen, C. and Pedersen, C. (2008). Older workers in Australia: The myths, the realities and the battle over workforce flexibility. *Journal of Management & Organization*, 14: 1, 73–84.

[41] Bayl-Smith, P. and Griffin, B. (2014). 'Age discrimination in the workplace: Identifying as a late-career worker

and its relationship with engagement and intended retirement age.' *Journal of Applied Social Psychology*, 44, 588–599.

[42] MacDonald, J. and Levy, S. (2016). 'Ageism in the workplace: The role of psychosocial factors in predicting job satisfaction, commitment and engagement.' *Journal of Social Issues*, 72: 1, 169– 90. doi:10.111.josi.12161

[43] Cheung, C., Kam, P., and Ngan, R. (2011). 'Age discrimination in the labour market from the perspectives of employers and older workers.' *International Social Work*, 54: 1, 118–136. doi:10.1177/0020872810372368

[44] O'Brien, K., Scheffer, M., van Nes, E., and van der Lee, R. (2015). 'How to break the cycle of low workforce diversity: A model for change.' *PLoS ONE*, 10: 7, 1–15. doi:10.1371/journal.pone.0133208

[45] Maurer, T., Barbiete, F., Weiss, E., and Lippstreu, M. (2008). 'New measures of stereotypical beliefs about older workers' ability and desire for development: Exploration among employees age 40 and over.' *Journal of Managerial Psychology*, 23, 395–418.

[46] Levy, B. (1996) as cited in Maurer, T., Barbiete, F., Weiss, E., and Lippstreu, M. (2008). 'New measures of stereotypical beliefs about older workers ability and desire for development: Exploration among employees age 40 and over.' *Journal of Managerial Psychology*, 23, 395–418.

[47] Billett, S., Dymock, D., Johnson, G., and Martin, G. (2011). 'Overcoming the paradox of employers' views about older workers.' *The International Journal of Human Resource Management*, 22: 6, 1248–1261. doi:10.1080/09585192.201 1.559097

[48] Australian Bureau of Statistics. (2016). Media release: Older workers finding more acceptance. Barriers and

Incentives to Labour Force Participation, Australia, July 2014 to June 2015 (Catalogue No. 6239.0). Retrieved from http://www.abs.gov.au/AUSSTATS/abs@.nsf/Previousproducts/6239.0Media%20Release1July%202014%20to%20June%202015?opendocument&tabname=Summary&prodno=6239.0&issue=July%202014%20to%20June%202015&num=&view= (accessed 23 July 2016).

[49] Steinberg, M., Donald, K., Najman, J., and Skerman, H. (1996). 'Attitudes of employees and employers towards older workers in a climate of anti-discrimination.' *Australian Journal on Ageing*, 15: 4, 154–158.

[50] Taylor, P., McLoughlin, C., Brooke, E., di Biase, T., and Steinberg, M. (2013). 'Managing older workers during a period of tight labour supply.' *Ageing & Society*, 33, 16–43. doi: 10.1017/S0144686X12000566

[51] Li, J., Duncan, A., and Miranti, R. (2015). 'Underemployment among mature-age workers in Australia.' *Economic Record*, 91: 295, 438–462. doi: 10.1111/1475-4932.12219

[52] Patrickson, M. (2016). 'Working and employability after 75 in Australia.' *Asia Pacific Journal of Human Resources*, 54, 188–206. doi: 10.1111/1744-7941.12090

Chapter 4

[1] Billett, S., Dymock, D., Johnson, G., and Martin, G. (2011). 'Overcoming the paradox of employers' views about older workers.' *The International Journal of Human Resource Management*, 22: 6, 1248–1261. doi:10.1080/09585192.2011.559097

[2] Schein, E. (1992) as cited in Appannah, A. and Biggs, S. (2015). 'Age-friendly organisations: The role of organisational culture and the participation of older workers.' *Journal of Social Work Practice*, 29: 1, 37–51.

[3] Bennington, L. and Tharenou, P. (1996). 'Older workers: Myths, evidence and implications for Australian managers.' *Asia Pacific Journal of Human Resources*, 34: 3, 63–76.

[4] Kulik, C. (2014). 'Spotlight on the context: How a stereotype threat framework might help organizations to attract and retain older workers.' *Industrial and Organizational Psychology*, 7: 3, 456–461.

[5] Greller, M. M. and Stroh, L. K. (1995) as cited in Perera, S., Sardeshmukh, K., and Kulik, C. (2015). 'In and out: Job exits of older workers.' *Asia Pacific Journal of Human Resources*, 53, 4–21. doi: 10.1111/1744-7941.12051

[6] Patrickson, M. and Ranzijn, R. (2004). 'Bounded choices in work and retirement in Australia.' *Employee Relations*, 26: 4, 422–432. doi:10.1108.014250410544515

[7] Ranzijn, R. (2004). 'Role ambiguity: Older workers in the demographic transition.' *Ageing International*, 29: 3, 281–308.

[8] Hennekam, S. and Herrbach, O. (2015). The influence of age-awareness versus general HRM practices on the retirement decision of older workers. *Personnel Review*, 44: 1, 3–21. DOI 10.1108/PR-01-2014-0031

[9] Skinner, N., Elton, J., Auer, J., and Pocock, B. (2014). 'Understanding and managing work-life interaction across the life course: A qualitative study.' *Asia Pacific Journal of Human Resources*, 52, 93–109. doi: 10.1111/1744-7941.12013

[10] Coupland, C., Tempest, S., and Barnatt, C. (2008). 'What are the implications of the new UK age discrimination

legislation for research and practice?' *Human Resource Management Journal*, 18: 4, 423–431.

[11] Harcourt, M., Wilkinson, A., and Wood, G. (2010). 'The effects of anti-age discrimination legislation: A comparative analysis.' *The International Journal of Comparative Labour Law and Industrial Relations*, 26: 4, 447–465.

[12] Patrickson, M. (2016). 'Working and employability after 75 in Australia.' *Asia Pacific Journal of Human Resources*, 54, 188–206. doi: 10.1111/1744-7941.12090

[13] Mountford, H. (2013). 'I'll take care of you: The use of supportive work practices to retain older workers.' *Asia Pacific Journal of Human Resources*, 51, 272–291.

[14] Perera, S., Sardeshmukh, K., and Kulik, C. (2015). 'In and out: Job exits of older workers.' *Asia Pacific Journal of Human Resources*, 53, 4–21. doi: 10.1111/1744-7941.12051

[15] Li, J., Duncan, A., and Miranti, R. (2015). 'Underemployment among mature-age workers in Australia.' *Economic Record*, 91: 295, 438–462. doi: 10.1111/1475-4932.12219

[16] McCausland, T., King, E., Bartholomew, L., Feyre, R., Ahmad, A., and Finkelstein, L. (2015). The technological age: The effects of perceived age in technology training. *Journal of Business and Psychology*, 30, 693–708. DOI 10.1007/s10869-014-9390-5

[17] Martin, G., Dymock, D., Billett, S., and Johnson, G. (2014). 'In the name of meritocracy: Managers' perceptions of policies and practices for training older workers.' *Ageing & Society*, 34, 992–1018. doi:10.1017/S0144686X12001432

[18] Parry, E. and Urwin, P. (2011). 'Generational differences in work values: A review of theory and evidence.'

International Journal of Management Reviews, 13, 79–96. doi:10.1111/j.1468-2370.2010.00285.x

Chapter 5

[1] Christensen, H. (2001). 'What cognitive changes can be expected with normal ageing?' *Australian and New Zealand Journal of Psychiatry*, 35, 768–775. doi: 10.1046/j.1440-1614.2001.00966.x

[2] Brough, P., Johnson, G., Drummond, S., Pennisi, S., and Timms, C. (2011). 'Comparisons of cognitive ability and job attitudes of older and younger workers.' *Equality, Diversity and Inclusion: An International Journal*, 30: 2, 105–126. doi:10.1108/02610151111116508

[3] Patrickson, M. (2016). 'Working and employability after 75 in Australia.' *Asia Pacific Journal of Human Resources*, 54, 188–206. doi: 10.1111/1744-7941.12090

Appendix

Austin, M. and Droussitis, A. (2004) as cited in Wood, G., Wilkinson, A., & Harcourt, M. (2008). Age discrimination and working life: Perspectives and contestations – a review of the contemporary literature. *International Journal of Management Reviews*, 10: 4, 425–442.

Australian Human Rights Commission. (2008). Mature workers mean business. https://www.humanrights.gov.au/our-work/age-discrimination/publications/mature-workers-mean-business-2008 (accessed 19 June 2016).

Australian Human Rights Commission. (2015). National prevalence survey of age discrimination in the workplace. Author, Sydney.

Bennington, L. and Tharenou, P. (1996). 'Older workers: Myths, evidence and implications for Australian managers.' *Asia Pacific Journal of Human Resources*, 34: 3, 63–76.

Billett, S., Dymock, D., Johnson, G., and Martin, G. (2011). 'Overcoming the paradox of employers' views about older workers.' *The International Journal of Human Resource Management*, 22: 6, 1248–1261. doi:10.1080/09585192.2011.559097

Bittman, M., Flick, M., and Rice, J. (2001). *The recruitment of older Australian workers: A survey of employers in a high growth industry.* SPRC Report 6/01 Social Policy Research Centre University of New South Wales, Sydney.

Branine, M. and Glover, I. (1997) as cited in Wood, G., Wilkinson, A., & Harcourt, M. (2008). Age discrimination and working life: Perspectives and contestations – a review of the contemporary literature. *International Journal of Management Reviews*, 10: 4, 425–442.

Brough, P., Johnson, G., Drummond, S., Pennisi, S., and Timms, C. (2011). 'Comparisons of cognitive ability and job attitudes of older and younger workers.' *Equality, Diversity and Inclusion: An International Journal*, 30: 2, 105–126. doi:10.1108/02610151111116508

Capowski, G. (1994) as cited in Bennington, L. and Tharenou, P. (1996). 'Older workers: Myths, evidence and implications for Australian managers.' *Asia Pacific Journal of Human Resources*, 34: 3, 63–76.

Capowski, G. (1994) as cited in Maurer, T., Barbiete, F., Weiss, E., and Lippstreu, M. (2008). 'New measures of stereotypical beliefs about older workers' ability and desire for development: Exploration among employees age 40 and over.' *Journal of Managerial Psychology*, 23, 395–418.

Cheung, C., Kam, P., and Ngan, R. (2011). 'Age discrimination in the labour market from the perspectives of employers and older workers.' *International Social Work*, 54: 1, 118–136. doi:10.1177/0020872810372368

Coupland, C., Tempest, S., and Barnatt, C. (2008). 'What are the implications of the new UK age discrimination legislation for research and practice?' *Human Resource Management Journal*, 18: 4, 423–431.

Fossum, J.A., Arvey, R.D., Paradise, C.A. and Robbins, N.E. (1986) as cited in Kooij, D., de Lange, A., Jansen, P., and Dikkers, J. (2007). 'Older workers motivation to continue to work: Five meanings of age. A conceptual view.' *Journal of Managerial Psychology*, 23: 4, 364–394.

Gibson, K.J., Zerbe, W.J. and Franken, R.E. (1992) as cited in Bennington, L. and Tharenou, P. (1996). 'Older workers: Myths, evidence and implications for Australian managers.' *Asia Pacific Journal of Human Resources*, 34: 3, 63–76.

Harcourt, M., Wilkinson, A., and Wood, G. (2010). 'The effects of anti-age discrimination legislation: A comparative analysis.' *The International Journal of Comparative Labour Law and Industrial Relations*, 26: 4, 447–465.

Heyma, A. and Nauta, A. (2014). 'What makes older job-seekers attractive to employers?' *De Economist*, 162, 397–414. doi:10.1007/s10645-014-9239-3

Hornstein, Z., Encel, S., Gunderson, M. and Neumark, D. (2001) as cited in Wood, G., Wilkinson, A., & Harcourt, M. (2008). Age discrimination and working life: Perspectives and contestations – a review of the contemporary literature. *International Journal of Management Reviews*, 10: 4, 425–442.

Hummert, M. L. (1999) as cited in Kulik, C. (2014). 'Spotlight on the context: How a stereotype threat framework might help organizations to attract and retain older workers.' *Industrial and Organizational Psychology,* 7: 3, 456–461.

Kulik, C. (2014). 'Spotlight on the context: How a stereotype threat framework might help organizations to attract and retain older workers.' *Industrial and Organizational Psychology,* 7: 3, 456–461.

MacDermott, T. (2014). 'Older workers and extended workforce participation: Moving beyond the 'barriers to work' approach.' *International Journal of Discrimination and the Law,* 14: 2, 83–98. doi:10.1177/1358229113520211

Martin, G., Dymock, D., Billett, S., and Johnson, G. (2014). 'In the name of meritocracy: Managers' perceptions of policies and practices for training older workers.' *Ageing & Society,* 34, 992–1018. doi:10.1017/S0144686X12001432

McIntosh, B. (2001) as cited in Johnson, G., Billett, S., Dymock, D., and Martin, G. (2013). 'The discursive (re)positioning of older workers in Australian recruitment policy reform: An exemplary analysis of written and visual narratives.' *Equality, Diversity and Inclusion: An International Journal,* 32: 1, 4–21. doi:10.1108/02610151311305588

Nelson, T. (2016). 'The age of ageism.' *Journal of Social Issues,* 72: 1, 191–198. doi:10.1111.josi.12162

Ng, T. and Feldman, D. (2008). 'The relationship of age to ten dimensions of job performance.' *Journal of Applied Psychology,* 93: 2, 392–423. doi: 10.1037/0021-9010.93.2.392

Patrickson, M. and Ranzijn, R. (2004). 'Bounded choices in work and retirement in Australia.' *Employee Relations,* 26: 4, 422–432. doi:10.1108.014250410544515

Pickersgill, R., Briggs, C., Kitay, J., O'Keefe, S., and Gillezeau, A. (1996) as cited in Bittman, M., Flick, M., and Rice, J. (2001). *The recruitment of older Australian workers: A survey of employers in a high growth industry.* SPRC Report 6/01 Social Policy Research Centre University of New South Wales, Sydney.

Ranzijn, R. (2004). 'Role ambiguity: Older workers in the demographic transition.' *Ageing International,* 29: 3, 281–308.

Roberts, I. (2006). 'Taking age out of the workplace: Putting older workers back in?' *Work, Employment and Society,* 20: 1, 67–86. doi:10.1177/0950017006061274

Skinner, N., Elton, J., Auer, J., and Pocock, B. (2014). 'Understanding and managing work-life interaction across the life course: A qualitative study.' *Asia Pacific Journal of Human Resources,* 52, 93–109. doi: 10.1111/1744-7941.12013

Soldan, Z. and Nankervis, A. (2014). 'Employee perceptions of the effectiveness of diversity management in the Australian public service: Rhetoric and reality.' *Public Personnel Management,* 43: 4, 543. doi: 10.1177/0091026014533093

Steinberg, M., Donald, K., Najman, J., and Skerman, H. (1996). 'Attitudes of employees and employers towards older workers in a climate of anti-discrimination.' *Australian Journal on Ageing,* 15: 4, 154–158.

Taylor, P., McLoughlin, C., Brooke, E., di Biase, T., and Steinberg, M. (2013). 'Managing older workers during a period of tight labour supply.' *Ageing & Society,* 33, 16–43. doi: 10.1017/S0144686X12000566

Wood, G., Wilkinson, A., and Harcourt, M. (2008). 'Age discrimination and working life: Perspectives and contestations – a review of the contemporary literature.' *International Journal of Management Reviews*, 10: 4, 425–442.

Acknowledgements, with Thanks

It has only been possible to get this book to you with the help and support of many people – my family, my friends and colleagues, and the professionals who contributed their special expertise to the work.

I thank my father, Norman Shrubsole, for his valued advice and ongoing support through the development, review, design and publication of this book.

I also extend my thanks to Dr Eugene Toker and Valerie Toker for their advice and support through the concept development, the drafting process and the publication of this book.

For my friends and colleagues, Gayle White, Lynne Cawley and Nyrée Illingsworth, many thanks for your expert advice and valued personal support in helping me realise a long-held dream.

I would like to acknowledge and thank the professionals who worked so hard to put this book in your hands: Kirsty Ogden of Epiphany Editing & Publishing, and

Marcela Ramirez of MRPR Copywriting and Professional Communication.

I also wish to acknowledge the organisations and institutions that in various ways enabled the publication of this book:

The Arts Law Centre of Australia

The Queensland Writers Centre

Griffith University, where sections of this research were carried out while I was a student completing a Master of Employment Relations degree.

The Next Steps

Thank you for commencing this journey with me. I believe it is a journey because there's still lots to explore, learn and do. For updates on this book and to find out about my upcoming publications, please subscribe to my email list (prohaskahampton@gmail.com).

I would love the opportunity to further discuss these messages and action steps with local organisations, teams and community groups. Please email me if you are interested in engaging me for speaking appearances, conferences and workshops (prohaskahampton@gmail.com).

Finally, if you found something valuable in the journey through this book, please tell your colleagues and friends about the book, and share your thoughts by reviewing the book on Amazon.com.

Catherine S. Shrubsole

About the Author

Catherine S. Shrubsole is passionate about talent management. An experienced human resources practitioner, writer and speaker, she has been consulting, training and researching in human resources for more than twenty years. She holds a Bachelor of Commerce and a Bachelor of Arts (Honours) in Psychology from the University of Queensland, and a Master of Employment Relations.

Catherine knows first-hand the valuable contribution that older workers offer, and champions the benefits a diverse workforce can bring to business and the community as a whole.